Come Gather 'Round

TIME-TESTED LESSONS FROM A
LIFELONG CATECHIST

Time-tested lessons
from a lifelong **catechist**

CAROL CIMINO, SSJ, ED.D

TWENTY-THIRD PUBLICATIONS
A Division of Bayard
One Montauk Avenue, Suite 200
New London, CT 06320
(860) 437-3012 or (800) 321-0411
www.23rdpublications.com

Copyright ©2009 Carol Cimino, SSJ, Ed.D. All rights reserved. No part of this publication may be reproduced in any manner without prior written permission of the publisher. Write to the Permissions Editor.

The Scripture passages contained herein are from the *New Revised Standard Version of the Bible*, copyright ©1989, by the Division of Christian Education of the National Council of Churches in the U.S.A. All rights reserved.

ISBN 978-1-58595-770-5
Library of Congress Catalog Card Number: 2009933796
Printed in the U.S.A.

CONTENTS

Introduction		1
Chapter 1	Why this is important	5
Chapter 2	Words, words, words *The experience of the Word of God*	17
Chapter 3	All are welcome *The experience of community*	22
Chapter 4	Hold the herring juice *The experience of service*	31
Chapter 5	It's the same! *The experience of prayer and liturgy*	37
Chapter 6	Because I said so *The experience of orthodoxy*	47
Chapter 7	This is awesome! *The experience of the sacred*	53
Chapter 8	You want me to do what? *Challenges of the faith*	61
Chapter 9	A martini in a teacup	67
Chapter 10	Meet the parents	78
Afterword	Eight physical elements *…That make a huge difference in the classroom*	84
References		88

Introduction

It was Ash Wednesday and I was in a church waiting for Mass to begin. I was praying to know what would be asked of me this Lent; what would I be called on to do? As I sat in the middle of the pew, a mother with a severely disabled child sat in the pew to the right of me with the child in a wheelchair in the aisle. On the other end of the pew, to the left, came a woman with several black garbage bags; it was clear that she was a "street person," and that all of her belongings were included in the bags.

When the time came for the collection, my "bag lady" rummaged around her bags and came up with a change purse. Inside were a few dollar bills, and one five-dollar bill, which she drew out and placed in the collection basket. In the meantime, the little girl grew agitated and began mewling, while the mother kissed her face and talked with her soothingly. Bingo! Look around! God is at work! Pay attention to what is going on around you and see that God is present.

I never planned to be a teacher, and I have to admit that my students have taught me more than I have ever taught them. In fact, any teacher worth his or her salt will tell you the same thing. But it's the "beholding" that makes it awesome.

I am convinced that our young people simply want us to be present to their unfolding. As they fumble around trying to figure out why they exist, who God is, and why it's important to know this stuff, we teachers are privileged to watch them. I have been privileged to teach young people in Catholic schools and parish religious education programs since 1965. In that time, I have encountered thousands of young people, been witness to several hundred paradigm shifts, and come to the realization that standing in the front of a classroom expostulating on the truths of the Catholic faith just doesn't cut it. Youngsters need to have a "deep down" experience or set of experiences so that it's not all "book learning," but something else altogether.

As a public speaker, keynoter, trainer, and workshop presenter since 1987, I have given presentations all over the country, trying, in my fractured way, to help today's teachers to do the impossible: accompany young people on their journey of faith. This little book is the result of an encounter that I had in 2008 at the Los Angeles Catechetical Congress, when I was asked to put a presentation called "Keeping the Faith" into a book form. Hey, I am a presenter, not a writer, but this is my best effort at putting down everything I have learned.

As our students grow into adulthood, the relationship that they have with God and with the Church will have been formed by several factors; among them is the time they have spent with us, their teachers. The experience of having known us is huge in their religious formation, and the question is, how will their experience of us predicate that relationship? If we can provide for them a multiplicity of experiences, they will have had opportunities to cement their beliefs, inherit the rich traditions of the Catholic Church, and encounter the transcendent. Pay attention!

Carol Cimino, SSJ, Ed.D.

CHAPTER 1

Why this is important

"You'll shoot your eye out, Ralphie." This *leitmotif* of Jean Shepard's perennial favorite *A Christmas Story* illustrates what this little book is about. The movie is Shepard's reminiscences about growing up in the late 1940s and, as an eight-year-old, desperately wanting a Red Ryder BB gun. The repeated warning comes true on Christmas morning, when Ralphie, having received the coveted rifle, figuratively shoots his eye out.

Research on the modalities of how youngsters learn has concluded that it is overwhelmingly experiential. That is, learning is more effectively made per-

> *"Go, then, to all peoples everywhere, and make them my disciples."*
> MATTHEW 28:19

manent when the students are provided experiences and an opportunity for immediate application of the learning of facts, ideas, or concepts. Think of how many times some adult warned you that dire consequences would ensue for such and such a behavior: "Your face will stay that way. It'll stunt your growth. You'll shoot your eye out." But how many times did you say to yourself, "Maybe everyone else, but not me," until something untoward did happen? It's been said that experience is the best teacher. Yes, it is!

Moreover, since the publication of Howard Gardner's *Frames of Mind* (1983), the theory of multiple intelligences has gained and retained purchase in educational circles. This theory of many ways of knowing provides a framework for the experiences that ought to be provided to students. That includes kinesthetic modalities; that is, actually experiencing something. Think: How did you learn to drive a car? Water ski? Use a computer? It was all experiential.

Gardner's list of "intelligences" includes eight means of learning. Here they are, along with some thoughts on what they mean in your classroom.

1. The verbal, or literal, intelligence. This relates to speaking, reading, using words. Children who like to learn verbally are good listeners. They like word games and puzzles, love puns and playing with words, like to listen to stories, and use a lot of words to describe memories, or ideas.

> Experiences for these children should include Scripture stories, writing letters in the vein of St. Paul, making up verbal prayers, inventing word games, and investigating word meanings and usages. For example, my students

loved the story of Abraham and Sarah being visited by angels, who promise Abraham that, in a year, he will be the proud father of a son. In the meantime, Sarah, his wife, is hidden in a tent and laughing about it because she thinks she's too old to have a child. So the son is called Isaac: "She laughed."

2. Logical-mathematical. This relates to quantification, and children who are logical-mathematically inclined will have questions related to quantifying, such as "how long did it take?" or "How big was it?" or "How old is it?" But students who prefer this intelligence are also fond of schedules, calendars, and routines, and they will remind the teacher if the routine is not being followed in the correct sequence.

Experiences for these children should include drawing maps and diagrams of the journeys of St. Paul, researching how people measured things in Scripture (it took "eight days" to walk around the walls of Jericho), doing timelines, and building models to scale (see God's directions for ark-building to Noah). It can also include constructing a calendar of Church seasons, listing the order of the Mass, and drawing a timeline of the papacies.

3. Musical. This relates to having an affinity for learning musically like rhythm, timbre, tone, and pitch, and loving to sing songs as well as to listen to them. (Think about how you learned the alphabet). They remember seemingly unrelated facts by putting them to music or to a rhythm. That child who drives you crazy by tapping his pencil on the desk is probably telling you that he likes to learn musically.

This is the first intelligence with which humans are endowed. We know that babies in the womb recognize the parents' voices, and many expectant parents will put music on to soothe the pre-born child. In Luke's Gospel (1:39–42), when Mary comes to visit her cousin Elizabeth, the babe in her womb leaps for joy.

Children who like to learn musically should be allowed to sing, make up songs about Gospel stories, learn through songs or rhythmic poems, listen to ballads, and write poetry.

While this intelligence is in its ascendancy even before birth, it may lie dormant until adolescence, when it is of utmost importance to the young teen. That's why, beginning in middle school, the i-Pod is grafted onto their ears. Think: what is the "music of your life"? Probably the music you loved as a teenager. Introduce the seasons of the Church with the music of the season; use popular music to teach life lessons (there is a subscription service that does this and is printed in many diocesan papers).

4. Kinesthetic. This relates to your fidgeters, the movers, youngsters who want to manipulate items, get up from their seats, sway to music. Think about learning to drive a car, riding a bike, skiing, and dancing—none of these can be learned by reading about them or seeing a movie or even a demonstration. It has been said that practice makes perfect; but more importantly, practice makes *permanent*.

Children who like to learn kinesthetically should be encouraged to act out Gospel stories or morality plays, make up dances to liturgical music, build models of the temple of Jerusalem, or a chart of the journeys of Paul, or taste some of the food that Jesus might have eaten. Teachers complain that children won't sit still; let's not let them sit still. Getting them up and around, having them move, will engage them holistically. I believe that the author of the Hokey Pokey was right: "you put your *whole self* in, and that's what it's all about."

5. Spatial. This relates to interpreting pictures, charts, graphs, maps; it's about *show me and I will know*. Children who are spatial (not spacey) like to look at photos, PowerPoint presentations, films and DVDs, Web sites, Facebook, YouTube—they even like to watch their music (think music videos). We're dealing with perhaps the most visual generation ever, and most children are visual learners—that is, they would rather see what they need to learn than hear about it.

Teachers and catechists need to keep in mind the visual preferences of children who prefer the spatial intelligence. Inviting them to create Powerpoint presentations, bring in pictures to express ideas, and use charts, maps, and videos will satisfy this preference and help youngsters to learn abstract concepts. Be sure to use movies to teach (e.g., baptism, *The Miracle Worker*; Eucharist, *Soul Food*); these are the parables of our time. Take them to see plays and art exhibits; visit monasteries, churches. (Notice how the spatial and the kinesthetic interact.)

6. Interpersonal. Sometimes we call these children extraverts, or we cringe because they just can't do anything without talking about it. But children who prefer to learn interpersonally love to participate in brainstorming, cooperative groups, panels—anything to satisfy their need and preference for thinking out loud. Children who prefer the interpersonal intelligence love to talk about their opinions, their thoughts, and their stories. Usually these children will be the first to raise their hands, and they always have something to say.

> Teachers and catechists can meet these students' preferences by allowing them to participate in groups, teams, and any activity in which they can express themselves. A caveat: Teachers and catechists need to help these children to reflect and pause occasionally because their verbosity often can be thoughtless and can overwhelm those not so extraverted. Sometimes these youngsters can be too self-revealing and may need to curb their enthusiasm, but will truly enjoy being able to share their ideas. Remember that for young and older adolescents, everything has been reduced to relationship; they want to explore how people are in relation to each other, and where they stand. Moreover, the importance of relationship, especially, for a twelve-year-old, cannot be overstated; at a time when the middle school child is pulling away from home and family, the peer group takes on a new priority.

7. Intrapersonal. Sometimes these children are seen as introverted, or shy and quiet. Children who prefer the intrapersonal intelligence may be more prone to reflection, and may be seen as the strong, silent type. Introverted individuals, however, make great conversationalists comparable to the extraverted; the difference is that while the more extraverted children are more self-revealing, the introverted are less so. Children who prefer the intrapersonal intelligence love to keep diaries and journals, reflect on pieces of music or literature, prefer quiet meditation or centering prayer, and are frequently surprising in their introspection. They may get stifled in the classroom by the extraverts, who may dominate classroom discussions and have their raised hands answered first.

Teachers and catechists need to slow the pace of questions and ideas for the intrapersonals, giving them time to think within themselves. Assign journals and reflective pieces; give them opportunities to think or even to "zone out." Make accommodation for these children when assigning group work; this kind of activity may make them reluctant to participate. They will respond to time for reflection, and for the chance to use their imagination.

8. Natural. Originally, Gardner defined seven intelligences, but in 2002, although he had announced the definition of a *spiritual* intelligence, he came out with the delineation of a *natural* intelligence. In educational terms, we used to call this "global learning" because it relates to the desire to learn "in context." Children who ask questions such as "Why do we have to know this?" or "Will we have a test on this?" or "What does it have to do with anything?" are trying to put learning into some context to which they can relate. The wise teacher or catechist will try to answer these questions as material is introduced. For example, "We need to study the Beatitudes in order to get an idea of what Jesus meant when he talked about the Good News."

There are a couple of nuances to the preference for the natural intelligence. The first, of course is the need to provide a context or a content for the learning. The second is more nuanced, and it's the need for young people to carve out a "space" in which to learn. This is often evidenced by how the student organizes his or her material, desk, or work space so that it reflects the student's preference for certain surroundings. For example, some students will festoon their desks with statues or medals that will inspire them to do well in a test. Other times a student may prefer certain places in the classroom—near a window, for example, or the back of the room, or the periphery of a circle. Teachers need to be sensitive to this preference: It helps the student to place himself or herself in a place conducive to learning or even to comfort.

I happen to believe that there are other "intelligences"—preferences for learning that we need to consider. For example, I believe that there is a *spiritual intelligence*: "I know because I believe." Anyone watching youngsters on Christmas understands that Santa Claus is real and gives meaning to Christmas for them.

I also believe that there is a *sexual intelligence*; boys and girls learn differently; while girls usually want to know *that* something works, boys usually want to know *how* it works.

How about a moral intelligence? Or a humor intelligence? The wise teacher or catechist carefully observes the young people he or she is teaching. What are the preferences for each of my students, and how can I play into them by providing experiences that cater to those preferences? If we truly believe that each of our students is an individual, then we will individuate the learning experience. Remember: One size fits *one*.

There has been a movement among those who direct parish religious education programs to take the programs out of the classroom arrangement. Several parishes conduct classes and meetings in a home setting, but recent concerns about children's safety have slowed the trend. Many dioceses hold summer programs, in addition to vacation Bible schools, where students who are unwilling to attend weekly classes can come to a one-or two-week half-day program that is supposed to supplant the weekly meeting. As a longtime educator, I am skeptical of this arrangement because it does not account for a paced "unfolding" of a student's learning experience, nor does it accommodate your introverted students who need time to "marinate" in a concept.

This book explores the varied experiences that should be afforded youngsters, and that should include varied venues as well. The classroom, the parish church, an outdoor meeting place, a ministry venue, a field trip to a monastery or a church, a temple, or a mosque: all of these should be considered in order to vary the learning experience.

In his opening address to the Second Vatican Council on October 11, 1962, Pope John XXIII listed five hopes that he had for that historic meeting. Each one of them should resonate with catechists and teachers of religion. They are:

1. Do not be prophets of gloom.
2. Discover ways of teaching the faith more effectively.

3. Deepen the understanding of doctrine.
4. Use the medicine of mercy.
5. Seek unity within the Church, with Christians separated from Catholicism, with those of non-Christian religions, and with all men and women of good will.

The question, then, becomes, what kinds of experiential learnings are catechists, parents, and teachers to provide in order to imprint on the minds and hearts of young people the knowledge, zeal, and love of this Catholic faith? There are several areas in which those charged with evangelizing young people can find significant experiences: the Word of God, the Christian community, the call of service, the people of God, the nature of orthodoxy, the challenge of believing, the sense of the sacred, and meaningful prayer and liturgy. I believe that each of these areas is contained in Pope John XXIII's list.

When I encounter my former students (and they are shocked that I am not only still alive, but still kicking!), what they tell me about their reminiscences is the experiences they had. "I remember when you took us to the monastery and we got to see real monks." "I remember going on that retreat and we had to cook and clean up afterwards; it made me appreciate my Mom." "I remember delivering food baskets, and I got to understand what it meant to be poor." "I remember the day you had us find out the date of our baptism; we celebrated it like a birthday."

What follows in this book are the fruits of almost fifty years of being in and out of a classroom with young people. I have been a teacher for most of my life, and everything I know about teaching I learned from young people. They are infuriating, loving, questioning, naïve, savvy, and mysterious. Oftentimes I would just look at them while they were taking a test, or doing some busy work and wonder about the mystery of their faith. It made me want to be very careful of this fragile, yet powerful force within them; it made me want to be a part of this journey toward their greatest potential: to be people of God. The quote from Matthew at the head of this chapter indicates, from Jesus' words, that what we are doing is far from creating a generation of young people who can parse the minutest of theological points; the commission of Jesus is to make *disciples*, with all that that term implies. Moreover, the teacher or catechist needs to look within him or herself to test, not his or her worthiness, but the level of zeal and energy that the catechist or teacher brings to the job.

Warning: I am not a theologian or a Scripture scholar, or an expert in Church history. I am a teacher. It is in my bones and sinews and is the little engine that runs me. Better still, I am a teacher who has taught children about this faith that we hold dear, and that, I am sure, we would die for, but find it more appealing, and perhaps more challenging, to live for.

I thought about calling this book *Jabs for Jesus,* or *KOs for Christ*. When I was in high school in Rochester, New York, the boys' school around the block held the annual Mission Bouts. Yes, that's right: students met in a boxing ring and punched each other out, all to raise money for the foreign missions. My friends and I attended every year; unknowingly, we were supporting the Church in some far-off land by watching these young men pound the living heck out of each other. But I'll never forget it, and, I am sure, neither will they.

LESSON

By mining each of these areas for those experiences that are appropriate to young people, catechists, parents, and teachers can prove the adage that religion is more "caught than taught." We can provide for the next generation's testimony, so that when they reflect on their religious upbringing, they will have to say, "You had to be there."

TRY THIS

1. Consider a regular schedule of field trips for each level of instruction. Students today have rarely visited a convent or a monastery, or a gathering place for religious services of another denomination. Get them out in the community to see the need for service projects such as clean-up activities, or service to the hungry.

2. Plan lessons to include experiences in at least three of Gardner's eight intelligences each time the class meets. Design student assessments using the same intelligences.

3. Have students discuss with each other significant experiences that they may have had since the last meeting. What made it significant?

4. Ask students to design a PowerPoint presentation on significant events from their parents' and grandparents' lives and compare them to the significant events in their own lives.

5. Have students create a timeline comparing historical events, milestones in the history of the Church and the parish, and their own lives. Then ask them to make observations on the intersection of "big" events with their own lives.

CHAPTER 2

Words, words, words

The experience of the Word of God

My students were mounting the popular 1970s musical *Godspell* and one day as I sat in my office, one of my seniors asked if she could stop in. "I get it, I finally get it," she said.

"What do you get?" I asked.

"This gospel stuff," she replied. "When we got on stage and started actually singing and reciting dialogue from the gospels, I got it!"

Here was a girl who had been in Catholic school since she was five years old, and now, at the age of eighteen, had finally "got it." I think the "it" was the meaning and richness behind Jesus' words and deeds, and I think the "got"

> *"In the beginning was the Word, and the Word was with God, and the Word was God."*
>
> JOHN 1:1

was what it really meant. If it takes a feel-good musical to do it, so be it. Jesus used money, stories, and probably some popular music of the day to illustrate what he meant by the Kingdom of God. Can we do anything less?

My generation was not allowed to have Bibles in school; it was feared that, if we read the Scripture, we might do something rash with it, like use it to figure out the meaning of our own lives. So, instead of Bibles, we used a book called a *Bible History*; what that did was to teach us that the Bible really was history, and not that some of the events described therein might be allegorical, or a story as the author saw it. Thanks be to God that the Church has now made the liturgy of the Word to stand with the liturgy of the Eucharist, and there are three cycles of Sunday Scripture readings so that we get to hear different readings—and all in English! Moreover, most religious textbook series are now Lectionary-based, so that our children not only read Scripture, but get to discuss its meaning in their own lives.

Our Protestant brothers and sisters have had familiarity with Scripture for centuries, and their quoting it in the presence of Catholic kids sometimes confounds our students. It is not enough, however, for our students to be familiar with chapter and verse; they need to "get it." At one time, I had the task of preparing a class of parish religious education sophomores for the sacrament of confirmation. When I gave each of them a Bible, I decided to find out what they knew about it. "OK," I said, "the Bible is divided into two parts; does anyone know what they are?" A long pause, and finally: "Uh, Part One and Part Two?" And there was the gnashing of teeth—mine.

When I went out to teach, a wise teacher told me: "Always remember to teach with the newspaper in one hand and the Bible in the other." Our job is to make the Scriptures, and especially the Gospels *relevant*; that is to make them integral in the lives of our students.

In 1984 and in 1986, I was fortunate to be a part of a "sister dioceses" program between the diocese of Rochester, New York, and the Diocese of Tabasco, Mexico. We spent two summers in very primitive conditions in a part of Mexico near the Guatemalan border. These *campesinos* had no electricity or running water in their homes; indeed, their homes were stick huts with thatched roofs. But, oh, did they love the gospels!

Every evening during our stay, we had a Scripture service. The people sang, prayed, and a different man or woman each evening presented a talk on how the readings of the day influenced his or her life. I learned so much! Interestingly, the cycle of readings for the time that I spent with these people was all about planting and harvesting; this was what these *campesinos* knew best, and they enriched their work and their lives (and mine) by relating this backbreaking work to sowing and reaping the Word of God.

But the highlight of each summer was the competition presented by the various *rancherias*, or little settlements. Each of the villages chose a gospel story and then re-enacted it, to the delight of everyone. Once a winner was decided, the *fiesta* began. I was privileged to witness some of the most profound interpretations of parables and miracles because these people, poor as they were, understood the richness of the promise of the Gospel.

There is a wonderful high school in Cape Girardeau, Missouri, where the students have, literally, made Scripture an everyday happening. They have displayed Scripture quotes all around the school, making sure that the quote matches the identity of the place. For example, the foyer of the school has a large aquarium, and above it is the quote from Genesis: "Let the waters be filled with every kind of living being…so God created all the great sea monsters and all kinds of creatures that live in the water…" (Genesis 1:20–21). The quote in the cafeteria, of course, speaks of Jesus feeding the five thousand, and so on. One can only imagine how the Scripture is ingrained in these students' lives on an everyday basis.

LESSON

The Gospel really is the Good News. It was the source of hope and expectation for those folks in Tabasco who really didn't have much else. The youngsters whom we teach, for the most part, have a lot more in terms of material good than those people who touched my life so profoundly, but they truly yearned for the Kingdom of God that is promised in Jesus' words.

TRY THIS

1. During the last days of Advent, the Church prays the "O Antiphons." They describe the coming savior as "Key of David," "Rising Sun," etc. Have the students make and display the images of these antiphons to post with the Jesse Tree or Advent wreath.

2. Use the idea from the high school in Cape Girardeau, as discussed in this chapter, to decorate with Scripture quotes the places in the classroom or building that are used for your religious education program.
3. Have students write and perform modern versions of the gospel stories.
4. Ask students to read the next Sunday's liturgical readings and make up "homely homilies" as if they were going to preach.
5. Ask students to think of movies that incorporate Scripture stories. For example, *Close Encounters of the Third Kind* could be the story of Abraham, and *Cool Hand Luke* is definitely the Stations of the Cross.
6. Work with students' language arts teachers to use the literature that they are reading to incorporate into references to Scripture. For example, Graham Greene's *The Power and the Glory* has a central character that is a "Christ Figure." O. Henry's "The Gift of the Magi" is a good example, as is Knowles' *A Separate Peace*. In any case, there is a plethora of literature that students can mine for references to Scripture.
7. Have students study the use of Scripture quotes in presidential inaugural addresses.
8. Have middle school students choose a Scripture quote that will become their "motto" or mantra. Have them design a personal crest incorporating this motto.

CHAPTER 3

All are welcome

The experience of community

I knew I'd bitten off more than I could chew when I volunteered my sixth graders to do the school's Christmas program and then, just three days prior to the performance, completely lost my voice. Marilyn was probably one of the smartest kids I ever taught, but she was a pariah among the other students, not only because she was smart, but because she just didn't mingle well (and, I suspect, because she wasn't very attractive).

In the midst of my misery, Marilyn asked if she could finish up rehearsing for the program. I thought, "Right. This ought to be interesting." But I agreed.

> *"They were all of one mind and one heart."*
>
> ACTS 4:32

Not only did my students sing their hearts out, they followed her every direction. She had found her niche.

Years later I received a letter from this young woman, by then an adult. "Dear Sister," it began, "I have tried to write this letter a thousand times, but was just unable to do so....I really wasn't the most popular kid in class in sixth grade, but after the Christmas show, the other kids just liked me!" Marilyn went on to explain that there was a lot of trouble in her home and that she and her siblings blamed themselves for the turmoil and really couldn't have friends come to their house because of it. Working with the others in the class to save the Christmas program from disaster cemented the circle of friends she had always wanted.

As a cultural group, the American psyche is programmed to be pretty individualistic, but as Catholics, we are communal by nature, and so it should be in our classrooms, schools, and parish programs. "You're nobody till somebody loves you," crooned Dean Martin, and how true it is with students. Unfortunately, some are "looking for love in all the wrong places" and will do anything, even crazy things, to win it. Moreover, teachers and catechists may be uncomfortable when their sixth-, seventh-, and eighth-grade students start wanting to put their arms around them, or call them by their first name, or seek personal information about them. They want some kind of connection with someone who is important in their lives, but they go about it awkwardly. Teachers and catechists need to realize that they don't "cross the line" with these young people, but they help them to form relationships with the adults in their lives.

How wonderful for a youngster to know that he or she is always welcome in the classroom or the group that meets weekly for religious instruction. Unfortunately, we cannot always program kids to accept or even to like one another, but unless every young person feels that his or her gifts (or shortcomings) are encouraged and even needed, then we cannot even begin to explore with students what it means to be the Christian community.

Never have I felt this more profoundly than when, two years after I'd taught the sixth grade, I was moved to the eighth grade. Of course, that meant that I would be teaching the same students that I'd had two years before. At the end of that year, they would be graduating and I'd be moving on to another school.

For their eighth-grade trip, I made arrangements to take them to the pastor's place where there was a swimming pool, horses, and acres of land for them to explore. That evening, at a barbecue arranged by parents, they announced that they had a graduation gift for me, and presented me with a vase of flowers. Of course, I thought: "Two years with these kids and all I get is flowers?" Then they overturned the vase and out came nickels, dimes, quarters—in abundance. I gaped, and they explained that they had been collecting the money ever since Christmas.

Now, that Christmas, I had gone on break wearing a traditional habit. By the time I returned, my order had changed to a modified habit—with hair! As I stared at all this change, Brad announced, "Sister, we want you to buy a decent outfit!" And Eddie added, "Yeah, and you might want to get a decent hairdo, too." I did and I did, and I showed up at their graduation to their magnanimous approval.

I think that the sense of community, a sense of belonging to something greater than oneself, inspires young people. These kids grew up in the suburbs where they didn't experience the sense of a neighborhood, their parents didn't sit on the front stoop on a summer's evening and chat among themselves while watching the kids play in the streets, and they lived where you have to get into a car to go and borrow a cup of sugar from the neighbor.

Because teens, especially, tend to reduce everything to relationship, the experience of belonging becomes acute; hence, we have them joining gangs in droves. At international Catholic youth rallies, at the traditional youth day at the Archdiocese of Los Angeles Catechetical Congress, and special diocesan celebrations for young people, you can find energetic gatherings of young people whose sole identity with the groups is their Catholic faith.

In an article in *U.S. Catholic* titled "U Mass" (2009) the author describes her sense of belonging at a college liturgy held at 10 PM on a Sunday night. She writes, "When another student prayed for exactly what had been plaguing my mind, I realized I had the support of an entire close-knit congregation behind me."

Sadly, our parishes have a poor track record of involving our young people (they *are* a scary group!), and many have gone to other faiths because of their teen programs and "fellowship." Yet, they will attend Mass or participate in prayer experiences and retreats when they can be with their friends and classmates. I have come to the conclusion that, perhaps, our efforts could pay off if we just provided these experiences to youngsters, and pitched services to their level of need. I am very fortunate to belong to a parish where the Sunday homilies really are relevant to every age group, but that is, in my experience, a rare occurrence. If parishes don't have the resources to form youth groups, then the weekly religious education class should focus on this building of *esprit* among the students.

How can this happen? It is, admittedly, difficult when the religious education classes only meet once a week, for, say, thirty weeks, and at a time when students are tired from a day of school, or soccer practice, or basketball games, or whatever. One of our problems is finding time when they are not tired and facing the prospect of homework in between.

There are several parishes that sponsor "lockdowns"—the experience of spending an overnight at a parish facility: a gym or large gathering space. This can be done around a theme, perhaps a social justice topic, such as homelessness, or hunger, or immigration, or violence. Students gather on a Friday evening, hear a presentation or view a video on the topic, discuss the topic, come up with some personal solutions as well as societal or systemic solutions, and draw up a resolution for some personal and group action. In the meantime they are eating, doing some fun activities—anything but going to sleep—and this goes on all night long. I have been privileged to have been a part of a lockdown, and the kids loved it; I, on the other hand, was exhausted by the dawning of Saturday morning.

Much of what is contained in this chapter really relates to the teaching of teens—a time in their lives when they are at their most vulnerable and volatile, and the importance of belonging is most acute. Adolescents are so fragile, so vulnerable, that they need to be affirmed all the time. Irony escapes them; sarcasm or cynicism shut them down. Therefore, calling them pet names, or calling attention to their idiosyncrasies will only alienate them, and they will lose the sense of their value to the class and to the catechist. They are at a time when they are trying to pull away from their family, but desperately seeking another. Dr. Ron Taffel (2001) calls this the "second family." He describes it this way: "They [adolescents] surround themselves with friends, forming a second separate system.

As kids become more and more attached to their friends and to the common interests they share…it is a natural, easy step to divorce themselves not only from their first families, but from other significant adults as well."

In a later chapter I'll describe the kinds of adults that children need in the classroom. Suffice it to say, our young adolescents feel that they are not receiving the kind of attention they need.

When my niece was four years old, I did the "aunt" thing: I picked her up and took her to the zoo. Afterward, we went to the convent and I sat her down in the kitchen while I proceeded to make supper for the two of us.

Oh, how she prattled on! I never knew that a four-year-old could have so much to say. As I went from the stove to the sink to the refrigerator, she talked and I "uh-huhed." Finally she stopped. "Aunt Carol," she said. "You're not listening."

"Yes, I am, Dina. I'm even answering you."

"But you're not listening with your eyes!" she persisted. Then it dawned on me: she wanted "full-body listening."

While our children, especially our young adolescents, feel that they are not getting "full-body listening" at home, they will look for some other adult to lavish it on them; that may be us. Young teens, twelve- to fourteen-year-olds, want to be taken seriously, and want their views, opinions, hopes, and ideas heard. The wise catechist needs to be open to their often infuriating, information-starved opinions. The wise catechist needs to value their opinions: those opinions open a door into their minds. To dismiss their comments out of hand is to shut the door; it won't be opened again unless they open it, and we will have missed a great opportunity to explore what's really going on.

Younger children are much more resilient than we can imagine. But, more and more, they too are starved for genuine interest and attention. I have found that our children are jaded; they have experienced earlier what our generation experienced later. This includes being left alone, staying out all night, having members of the opposite sex spend the night, drinking alcohol, and traveling. In addition, our young children are jaded because everyone gets a trophy or an award, just for showing up. The result is that they are looking for rewards for doing nothing or rewards just aren't valued because they are come by cheaply. I remember attending a school awards ceremony. Several of the children had received certificates for a variety of things like being friendly or helpful. After the ceremony, I watched one of them throwing the certificates into the waste bin. "What are you doing?" I asked. "Just dumping these things; they really don't mean anything. I think my teachers just wanted to boost my self-esteem," was the reply.

Yes, students have built-in baloney detectors. What is genuine and real is taking a genuine and real interest in our students: listening to them, challenging their decisions, and showing that each of them is an integral part of the class.

I made it a point to learn all of my students' names before the second day of class. I also prided myself on learning the correct pronunciation of their names. When I taught in the minor seminary, I received a class list with the name Kacprczyk. "It doesn't have enough vowels," I thought. "How will I call the roll with this name?" Of course, I was worried that this group of eighteen-year-old boys (they were only five years younger than I) wouldn't accept my authority. As they piled into the classroom, I heard, "Hey Kaperzak [sic]! How was your summer?" Yes! Just as the Gospel of

Mark uses the words "awe and amazement," my students were awed and amazed when I correctly pronounced Stanley Kacprczk's name. And he just grinned.

The creation of the community of the classroom is crucial. Students need to know that they are valued and welcomed into this place. When they are noticed and made to understand that each of them brings a unique contribution to the group, they will understand this most basic belief that we have as Catholics, that we are the Body of Christ.

LESSON

When we say that everyone is welcome in our classes, we need to mean that EVERYONE is welcome.

TRY THIS

1. Have students research all of their names; what are their origins? Are they traditional family names? Ask them what name they would choose for themselves. How does that name describe who they are?

2. This is an old idea: have students list the names of everyone in the class on one side of a piece of paper. Opposite each student's name, list a positive quality of that person. Ask them to hand in these papers. Then cut them up, and give each student the collection of attributes that each student had contributed.

3. Establish rituals in the classroom. This creates a unique culture and cements the common experiences of the stu-

dents. I had a routine for the beginning of each class that consisted of thirty seconds of reflection on any needs that students had, and then a loud "Amen" from the class. At the end of class we did a communal blessing over each other to pray for a safe journey home and to meet again the next time. When I forgot this once, my students had to remind me. It signaled to me that this was important to them.

4. Do something fun. Once a year we celebrated everyone's birthday, and students told what made family celebrations of birthdays special. When I taught school, we held a "Beautiful Day" celebration every year during the dark, ugly month of February. Students dressed in their finest, and we did only beautiful things that day in class. I still run into those kids (thity-eight years later) who will mention Beautiful Day.

5. Work with students to choose a class theme for the year, complete with a symbol and a mantra or model. Use this theme for the opening and closing prayer each time the class meets.

CHAPTER 4

Hold the herring juice

The experience of service

The idea of service projects didn't occur to me until I watched a youngster running out the door to catch the school bus. As he grabbed his school bag he yelled to his mother, "Mom, I need a canned good for the food collection!" She went to the cupboard to get an item that she had harbored for many years, in heartfelt anticipation of just such an occasion: the can of herring juice.

Anyhow, that's what was tossed to the young man, and off he went to do his service: tossing that can of herring juice into the box for the collection. And voila! A service project!

Years ago I took a carload of high

> *"Go sell all that you have and give it to the poor, for you will have riches in heaven."*
>
> MARK 10:21

school students to the scene of a devastating flood. We slept on the floor of the local high school gym, and we were sent out as a small group each day to a house or a neighborhood to see what help we could give to the folks that had been victims of the flood. What amazed the kids was that people didn't want valuables, or furniture pulled out of their devastated homes; it was the family photo albums. Our discussions about the day's work revealed that they had come to realize what's really important in life—family, memories, tangible reminders of the intangible. That was over thirty years ago, and my former students still mention it when I see them.

In Catholic schools and parish religious education programs, we do *Christian* service. There's something different about that. It is different from doing service projects for a merit badge, or to look good on a resume. We do service because that is what our faith tells us: "Unless you do good works, your faith is dead," writes James in his letter in the New Testament.

But I am convinced that sometimes our students don't get the fact that we do service for others, and not just for ourselves.

A number of years ago, I took some high school girls with me to deliver the food baskets that they had collected. As we arrived in front of a house, I told them to ring the doorbell and then take the box of food into the house, when the woman answered the door. When they came back out, they were angry: "She didn't even thank us," they complained. That was my first clue: "Don't you know that this wasn't about you?" I asked. "This was about her, and the fact that she needs what we can give."

Too often, I think, our students approach their service from a sense of power: We have and you don't, and we'll give you something because we can. I've learned that when we give young people the experience of doing service, we adults need to contextualize it: Service is our call as baptized persons, we do it because we are responsible for others, and it should impel us to do more.

In practical terms, we need to explain to our youngsters the context of service: Jesus, tired after a long day, cures Peter's mother-in-law; having been the beneficiary of this service, she leaps out of bed and begins to serve dinner. After dinner, according to Mark's Gospel, the crowds come around to ask Jesus for more healing. It's a kind of "pay it forward" principle. (Of course, no one asked Peter if he even wanted his mother-in-law cured.)

Christian service also teaches our young people about personal responsibility, and this needs to be explored with them. I had a young woman come to class to ask why we were writing letters for Amnesty International to urge a foreign country to release political prisoners. "Why do I have to do this? I don't even know these people!" That reminded me of my mother's attempts to make me eat my veggies. "Think of the starving millions," she would say. And I would say, "Name five." This did not sit well with her, and I spent a lot of time being grounded. But I've learned that personal responsibility for other human beings comes out of our belief in the universal Body of Christ. In the words of Paul, "if one part of the body isn't functioning, then the whole body suffers."

What kind of involvement is required to do real Christian service? Simply collecting canned goods, or cooking a meal, or collecting money for some cause is perfunctory involvement. But what about discussing how to deliver it? What it will mean to the families who are the recipients? How about coming back and reflecting and praying about how the little we do makes a difference in people's lives? What about our global responsibility?

I am appalled, at times, by our students' ignorance of history, geography, and world events. The current inclination to take care of ourselves and our own is not at the heart of Christian service. Jesus' conversation with the Canaanite woman confirms this. Even though Jesus is reluctant to grant her wish, it is not only her persistence, but the fact that she represents "Everywoman" who has ever had a sick child and would go to the mat for that child. In other words, our service should not be xenophobic, or confined to those whom we know. The catechist or the teacher cannot merely bring the classroom into the world, so he or she needs to bring the world into the classroom.

Often, it is not the youngsters who stymie efforts at real service. When I taught high school sophomores in the parish faith formation program, we planned on cooking and serving a dinner at one of the local soup kitchens. I was so excited that we were going to do this, because I thought it would be an experience that would solidify a sense of community among the kids. As the day approached, however, various members of the class started backing out, until only a couple of them and I were left cooking a turkey dinner and bringing it downtown to serve. The problem? Their parents didn't want them going to "that" part of town, and being with "those" people.

That was the downside. The upside was that the kids who stuck with it excitedly told of their experiences at the following week's class. The consensus: "Those people are real, and they aren't weird or dangerous." One of the students even said that one of the guys reminded her of her grandfather, and when she talked with him during dinner, he showed her pictures of his grandchildren. "I guess they have families, too," she concluded. "They just can't stay in one place."

One year, during Lent, I asked seventh-grade students to bring in pictures from magazines and newspapers to illustrate our own Stations of the Cross. I was pleasantly surprised when they brought in so many pictures from the then-festering war in Vietnam. The pictures of people affected by that seemingly never-ending war really touched them, and they were able to relate what was going on on the other side of the world to the suffering of Jesus. What a great lesson in compassion! We started working with a local parish that was resettling the Montagnards and other Catholic Vietnamese refugees.

As one looks at the numbers of young people joining the Jesuit volunteers, or Notre Dame University Alliance for Catholic Education (ACE) or the LaLanne Program out of the University of Dayton, it is clear that young people want to be of service, especially in the Church. A recent survey by the Center for Applied Research in the Apostolate (CARA) concluded that today's youth are a generation in search of a cause. After all, their parents can tell them about the protests of the Vietnam era, the grape boycotts, and the civil rights marches; what is their cause? What can cement their identity as a generation?

Today's young people are generous and good-hearted. Our job as teachers and catechists is to harness that generosity and good-heartedness, and place it in the context of the holistic Christian life. Remember that, for our young adolescents, relationship is everything; put a face on need, and they'll go the extra mile for that person. The relief effort for the victims of Hurricane Katrina in 2005 proved that: when kids made contact with actual people, they were generous to a fault. Finally, young people need to have the experience of reflecting on their actions so that their service, unlike the herring juice, becomes something real, valuable, and, most of all, memorable.

LESSON

Herring juice does not a Christian service make.

TRY THIS

1. Ask young students to list what their household chores are and to determine what a big help they are to their parents.
2. Discuss some needs of the parish: Do the parish grounds need some cleaning up or beautification? Perhaps a fall and spring clean-up day can be organized by students.
3. Instead of collecting food baskets at holiday times when everyone is doing this, pick another time of the year to restock the shelves of the local food bank.
4. Host a "senior prom" where the local senior citizens are the guests of your older (grade 8 and up) students. Provide some "oldies" music and have students dance with the seniors.
5. Use Valentine's Day or St. Nicholas Day to do something nice for special people in the parish, like baking cookies or making "goodie bags" for shut-ins or sick persons. Items such as sample-size shampoo, lotions, bath gels, and sewing kits are appreciated.
6. Ask students to create a service calendar, where they list dates of regular service, so that service projects don't become once-a-year events, but part of their regular lives. The calendar should list service at home, in the neighborhood, in the parish, in the student's school, and even in the world.

CHAPTER 5

It's the same!

The experience of prayer and liturgy

For twenty-two years, I took high school students to Europe, usually during Holy Week and Easter Week. What possessed me to undertake this exercise in futility, I will never know, but it allowed me the experience of being with kids outside of school (I am still not even sure that this was a good thing, since I know I aged fifty years doing it).

So, on one trip, we're standing in St. Peter's Square attending the Papal Mass and behind me I can hear, in a stage whisper, "Sister! Sister!" This goes on until the young man gets to my side. "Sister!" "Yes, Steven?" I say (this

> *"This, then, is how you should pray. Our Father in heaven: May your holy name be honored."*
>
> MATTHEW 6:9

ought to be good). He points to the altar and exclaims, "It's the same! The Mass! It's the same!"

Revelations like this are few and far between, but when they occur, they last a lifetime. Steven had just figured out something about the Church universal and couldn't wait to share it.

Too many young people, especially teens, present a real challenge when it comes to regular attendance at the Eucharistic liturgy. They can't figure out why they should have to go; can't they just pray in their room? On the other hand, if teens begged to attend Mass on the weekend, or used every means in their arsenal to get to Church on Sunday, how would parents spend their time and energy? Sadly, recent findings by CARA show that this generation of students has a fifteen percent church attendance rate, one-half of that of the generation ahead of them.

So, how to give students the experience of a liturgy that truly moves them? With the dearth of priests available for youth liturgies, we need to get creative. I'm going to take some heat on this, but how about bringing back the children's Mass on Sunday? Why not have a Sunday evening Mass? The experience of late Sunday evening Masses at Newman Centers proves that young people will attend Mass when its schedule conforms to their own body clocks.

But more than that, the Mass needs to provide something; the current lawsuits and movement to get God out of public schools' athletic events has pointed out one thing: kids want God in their lives. The parent tape comes to mind: "You have to go to church." "But I don't get anything out of it!" "You can't get anything out of it unless you put something into it. Besides, it's not about getting something." NOT!

Attend a youth Mass and you see kids making the music, doing the readings, standing around the altar, giving the welcome, and being treated to a homily that's often pitch-perfect. There's fellowship (a word used by persons of other faiths, but rarely for Catholics). Get something? You bet! Our young people need to be as comfortable in church as they are in their living rooms.

Having said that, however, the difficult part is to transcend the fellowship: Meeting friends is one thing; meeting God is quite another. We have the same challenge with teen retreats; they love being with each other, but the being "with God" is something else. Let's make youth liturgies a model of the Transfiguration; what you see is less than what you get. It is good for us to be here, not just together, but together to come to God, whose relationship with us is the whole purpose of coming together. Let's have dedicated youth Masses at various times. Our young people will respond to what truly stirs them; and they will come back for more.

There is a current phenomenon that should not be ignored. We have a sizeable number of young people, adolescents, usually, who are attracted to the Tridentine rite of the liturgy. What I think is happening is that we have some young people who are looking for something sacred, transcendent, and, most of all, mysterious in the Eucharistic celebration. If we pass up this opportunity to explore with them the profundity of the Eucharist, we will have missed a rare chance with them.

Of course, the current priest shortage has to be confronted. Teachers and catechists complain that they can't find a priest to celebrate a class or group Mass; it's understandable given the current dearth of celebrants. However, we have plenty of deacons who can conduct prayer and even Communion services, and who may be more available to young people and provide a vocation opportunity, too. Furthermore, children can encounter God in a really great prayer experience, or a service project, or a reflection on a Gospel story. While the Eucharistic liturgy remains the ideal, we need to explore other means at our disposal.

Now, what about prayer? We ought to teach young people that there are four reasons to pray: please, thank you, whoops, and WOW! This covers just about everything. I said this in class one day, and a girl quipped, "So, you mean we should pray all the time." "Good one," said I. A breakthrough!

Youngsters ought to be given the instruction and experience of different forms of prayer. Simply reading a prayer or a piece of inspirational writing won't cut it with a generation that has learned to be jaded or suspicious of structure and rules. After all, many of them have concocted their own mélange of religion: a dash of Zen, a dollop of Buddhism, a pinch of self-help, and voila: a religion (today: tomorrow, it's something else, perhaps having to do with being vegan).

We also need to pay more attention to the value of reflection and meditation; I think that teachers and catechists sometimes focus on filling in silence with words. And, yet, isn't it our job to let our students know that they should be comfortable with God in the silence? Several years ago, PBS aired a special on former prisoners of war. They had an ex-POW from World War II, a guy from the Korean War, and an ex-pilot from Vietnam who had been held prisoner in the "Hanoi Hilton" for eight years.

"What kept you going?" asked the interviewer of the Vietnam POW. "Was it thoughts of your family? Hope that you would be rescued?" "Neither," answered the GI. "The nuns taught me how to meditate when I was in Catholic school, and, in the silence, I placed myself firmly in God's love. That's what kept me going." Wow.

Encouraging students to use their inner selves to encounter God, or helping them to pray with Scripture or to use a journal to express their ineffable encounters with the Divine ought to be interspersed with rote or spoken prayer. If God isn't limited in the media through which we encounter the Creator, then why should we limit students' routes to God?

This is a good time to bring up the Church or liturgical year. The rhythm of the annual observances of the history and happenings of our Church is a great opportunity to teach prayer and liturgy in the classroom and beyond. I use the song "Seasons of Love" from the musical *Rent*. The song is about the 525,600 minutes of the year, and asks, "How do you measure a year? Oh you got to remember the love, you know that love is a gift from up above…measure, measure your life in love."

The liturgical year offers a plethora of opportunities for teaching and living a special calendar—one that follows the life of Jesus, Mary, and the saints. Students should understand that the Church calendar was crafted at a time when people didn't own calendars or clocks. Special feasts invited people to interrupt their daily lives for special celebrations, and the constant wars and fighting were suspended on these days, thus saving countless lives and property. There are some beautiful renderings of the cycle of the liturgical year available; students should be provided with their own copy, or at least a template that they can fill in. Bulletin boards, PowerPoint presentations, internet visits to different parts of the world to observe how feasts are celebrated around the globe—all of these are great ways to teach that, besides the civil year, there is the calendar that invites us to celebrate with the universal Church.

Of special note is a seldom-celebrated triduum of the Church: Halloween, the Feast of All Saints, and the Feast of All Souls. Mention Halloween to teachers and catechists, and they just shake their heads; this is the hardest holiday of the year for a couple of reasons: The kids are in class, and they want to dress up and party.

I have seen some really cute costumes: Spiderman, Dora the Explorer, Snoopy, and some really horrible ones—a six-year-old girl dressed as a French maid, complete with fishnet stockings, an eight-year-old boy as a pimp, young adolescents as their favorite punk rocker….Many parish faith formation programs invite students to dress as their favorite saint, or patron saint, and that's very instructive, very nice. But Halloween is a wonderful opportunity to teach kids about the subsequent feasts: All Saints and All Souls. In particular, Latin Americans pay special attention to the Día de los Muertos—the Day of the Dead. Children can learn a lot from studying this very popular celebration.

In an earlier chapter I wrote about the experience of a community, and how young people want to belong. The three aforementioned observances invite youngsters into a bigger, more spectacular community, one that is peopled with friends and strangers, past, present, and future. In other words, Halloween should be the beginning of a longer celebration that observes a cosmic community.

I would invite students to dress up as their favorite person, past, present, and future. Often they would come as they want to be, not as they were. This was a great chance to discuss choices that they would need to make in order to make their future selves become real. We talked about loved ones who had died, and how they lived in their hearts, and how they were probably saints, just not official ones.

Halloween invites children to confront scary things that go "bump in the night" and, eventually, to laugh at them. Halloween invites children to partake in ancient rituals that, in centuries past, pushed back the night and enabled people of faith to acknowledge their fears of demons and devils and to understand that the saints, particularly the martyrs, confronted these fears, too. Finally, Halloween is the threshold that invites children to pray for the dearly departed, especially those whom they miss very much. It puts our children in the middle of this Communion of Saints where everyone is welcome.

The readings at the end of the Ordinary Time between Pentecost and the first Sunday of Advent provide for wonderful discussions, as they tell of the "end of days." Kids are always interested in the end of the world, and they have feasted on a multitude of movies and TV programs that purport to show the end times. Of course, this time of year asks us to be prepared for the coming of the Lord to judge all of us. But it provides us a great discussion topic, especially with young adolescents, who, at this stage of their lives are capable of some serious introspection.

A 2009 Pew Trust research project uncovered a major reason for adolescents' risky behavior: They think that their lives will be cut short. When they look at the early demise of some of their rock star heroes: Michael Jackson, Kurt Cobain, even Princess Diana, they see idealized lives ended early by tragedy. Of course, we need to give these youngsters hope, but the end of Ordinary Time gives us a marvelous opportunity to discuss what it means to "Be Prepared."

The first Monday of Advent my classes celebrated the new year of the Church. I brought in noisemakers, and we wore the silly hats, and toasted each other with cranberry juice. It sounds silly, but it made a lasting impression on them, even though they thought I was nuts.

On Pentecost we sang "Happy Birthday" to the Church, and during Lent, an ugly time, weather-wise in the Northeast, as I mentioned earlier, we celebrated "Beautiful Day," where I asked the students to show up in their finest and we did beautiful things, like a slide show of flowers, or sharing a delicious treat, or listening to beautiful music or poetry—whatever would brighten up the season and express our hope in a season of love. It may have been an unorthodox way of celebrating the Church year, but it stuck.

The Church year is a wonderful tool that we can use to draw our students into the rhythm of the Church, the lives of Jesus and Mary, and the saints and solemnities. When I was a novice, we always had biscuits and honey on the feast of St. Francis de Sales, who said, "You will catch more souls with a teaspoon of honey than with a barrel of vinegar." We had pancakes and bacon on Mardi Gras, as we bade farewell to meat (*Carnevale*), we took the place of the superiors on the feast of the Holy Innocents, wore funny hats on the feast of St. Genevieve (although the headdress of the habit was funny enough), attended St. Joseph tables, and had breakfast standing up on Good Friday. There are as many customs and observances that vary with the ethnic and historical observances as there are saints. If, forty years later, I can still remember these customs and practices, so will your students.

LESSON

When they call your name in Rome, it pays to listen.

TRY THIS

1. Ask students to interview older relatives to discover how feasts and holy days were celebrated in the "old days."

2. Have students keep a journal of the Church year: Record the date of the liturgical season and describe what the student or the class did to observe it.

3. Ask students to take photos of their favorite statues or shrines; what is the history behind the memorial? Construct a bulletin board with the results. Ask students to research the history of famous churches like Notre Dame in Paris, St. Patrick's in New York, etc.

4. Have students research the history of the Mass: what is the origin of the vestments? How did the Mass get into its present form? What were the early Masses like? How is Mass celebrated in the rest of the world? Ask the pastor or the deacon to conduct a tour of the parish church; many First Communion classes do this.

5. Take students to a Mass that includes a different ethnic group: How is it similar to their experience? Different?

6. Use some of the ideas for observances of feasts that are described in this chapter. Ask students to research some of the traditions and put together a PowerPoint presentation for sharing with the other grades.

7. Here's a story to share: The family was supposed to go to Mass together, but the father of the family decided that it was too cold for him to go out to church, so the mother and the children went. When he looked outside, he noticed a small bird trying to get into the house and he concluded that he had to help the bird, so he went out and opened the barn so that the bird could be out of the elements, but the bird wouldn't enter the barn. He lit a lamp, figuring that the light would attract the bird, but, no luck. He put out some birdseed, and still, the bird wouldn't go into the shelter of the barn. Finally he thought, "If only I could become a bird, I could lead the bird into the barn." And then it struck him. This was why Jesus had come to earth, to show us the way. As he jumped into his car, he hoped that he could catch up with the family at Mass.

CHAPTER 6

Because I said so

The experience of orthodoxy

Words fail to express the jaw-clenching, head-throbbing, gut-heaving experience of giving directions to youngsters in a classroom.

"What page was that?"
"How many words do you want?"
"In our notebook?"
"Does it count?"
"Will we have a test on this?"

Well, you get the drift.

It seems to me that all of these questions, while destined to drive even the most calm of us to the brink of insanity (and beyond!), are really young people's attempts at defining what is expected, at discerning the boundaries

> *"The young man asked, 'What can I do to gain eternal life?' Jesus replied, 'Keep the commandments if you want eternal life.'"*
>
> MATTHEW 19:16–17

for themselves. Lucky for us, Catholic Church teaching, orthodoxy, provides clear boundaries in which our students can find their niche, while encouraging them to ask questions, internalize answers, and affirm their beliefs. The clear explanation of the Church's teachings in various moral areas can provide some semblance of certitude for young people who come from a culture with very little that is certain. Current areas of disagreement in our society such as the death penalty, euthanasia, abortion, the economy, world peace, and migration of peoples have been tackled by the leadership of the Catholic Church and clearly explored in light of the ongoing *leitmotif* of life.

Although many adults have some quibble with Church teaching (hey, it wouldn't be the Church if they didn't!) young people simply don't. They have grown up in a post-Vatican Church and have not experienced "Old Church vs. New Church." In fact, many of them want what we gave up in the '60s.

I see young people, especially high school students, who want tangible evidence of their faith. Although this seems like an oxymoron, I think it means that they want "stuff" like sacramentals; sacramentals help to solidify those boundaries described above. Why else would they be wearing scapulars, medals, and even tee shirts with "Catholic and Proud of It" on the front? We Catholics are the originals when it comes to "stuff." Let's give them holy water, incense, holy cards, medals, scapulars—all the tangibles they want.

When I was in school, the teaching of religion was all "head." Memorization of the Baltimore Catechism was the goal of religion classes. Bible reading was discouraged. At Mass, Scripture was read in Latin, so you buried your nose in your missal to get it in English. It was believed that, if you knew the facts of the faith, you would "know" the faith.

The 1960s swung (literally) in the opposite direction. All you needed to know was that Jesus loves you. We went from all "head" to all "heart," and, as a result, we have a whole generation of Catholics who are ignorant of the teachings of the Church.

The current generation of youngsters should be given equal doses of "head" and "heart." I once was teaching an American history class having to do with the African-American experience in America. I listed some terms, including "soul food." When I asked the class what it was, a young man called out, "Eucharist!" He then proceeded to explain to me that Jesus wanted us to follow his example: Nourish your body, but nourish your soul. What a great exposition of "head" and "heart."

Happily, catechists and Catholic schoolteachers have endless opportunities to learn the tenets of our faith. The *Catechism of the Catholic Church* and the *National Directory on Catechesis* offer definitions, explanations, and references to both Scripture and Tradition. Seminars, workshops, and speakers are available to explain the teachings of the Church; these are provided by dioceses and parishes, as well as such organizations as the National Conference for Catechetical Leadership (NCCL) or the National Parish Catechetical Directors (NPCD), who also organize annual conferences for renewal and getting reacquainted with the latest catechetical practice. Of particular note is the annual Los Angeles Catechetical Congress, which gathers some 35,000 teachers, catechists, youth ministers, and pastoral associates in Anaheim, California, each year. Add all this to the pages of documents and pastoral letters from the United States Conference of Catholic Bishops (USCCB), Vatican offices, and individual bishops, and there is no excuse for a teacher's or catechist's ignorance of Church doctrine.

If I have learned anything from students, it's that they want to know the rules. Now, one of the things that frustrates us is that young people, especially adolescents, have this uncanny ability to slice and dice what they will accept. I vividly remember the utter joy and love that teens showed Pope John Paul II. I was with a group of high schoolers in St. Peter's Square when the Pope appeared. *"Juan Pablo Secondo; ti chiere todo el mondo!"* they shouted, and my kids, with their own rudimentary Italian joined in the shouting.

"So," I said to them afterward, "you really like this pope."

"Yeah," they responded. "We just don't like some of his teachings."

"Which ones?" I persisted.

"You know, like living together before marriage, and birth control, and divorce, and holy days of obligation, and having to go to Mass on Sundays," they answered.

"Great," I said. "I'm glad you're at least happy with original sin."

After a moment of thought: "Ummmm...we have to think about that one, too." See what I mean?

With young children, there is, happily, a ready acceptance for the rules. Once they know the rules, they feel more in charge of their lives. Watch them on the playground: of course, for boys this means running—no purpose to it, mind you, but they run; it's the rule. But watch the girls: They will spend the whole of recess making up rules to some game that they will never play! But the rules are the game.

All of the ardor for the faith has to come out of the acceptance of Catholicism as "the whole ball of wax." I had to remind my students that, even when they really like someone or something, there's almost always something they don't like about that person or thing. For example, their best friends or even their parents might have some attributes that are undesirable, but they love them anyway.

Here was my definition for a friend: it's someone who knows you through and through and loves you in spite of all that. It comes down to how much you want something; are you willing to make sacrifices in order to have something that is valuable and meaningful in your life?

Often, especially with my high school students, we would look at scenes in the gospels where Jesus had to follow some rule. We see that Jesus paid the Temple tax, observed the Sabbath, and respected the Torah. He parsed some of the extrinsic practices that had crept into Judaism, such as the vendors in the Temple, the imposition of harsh practices on the people, and the hypocrisy of some of the religious leaders, but he didn't question the core tenets of the faith he practiced.

One of the results of the deliberations of the Second Vatican Council was the proclamation of the freedom of conscience, so clearly enunciated by the late great John Courtney Murray. Given this, our task is to help shape the consciences of our students so that they will acknowledge that the basic tenets of the Church are divinely handed down, have a basis in the life and teachings of Jesus, and help us to live "within the lines."

LESSON

Mind the rules.

TRY THIS

1. Have students gather some controversial news articles that might deal with issues such as immigration, stem cell

research, the death penalty. Have them do a web search for documents from the USCCB on these issues and discuss them in class.

2. Have students read the Precepts of the Catholic Church and compare and contrast them with the Five Pillars of Islam. Create a chart of comparisons and contrasts.

3. Ask students what teachings of the Church they hear others talk about, and why these are important issues for the Church.

4. Ask students to do a web search of all the councils of the Church. What issues did they deal with? Are these "burning issues" today?

5. Have older students examine the *Catechism of the Catholic Church*. Ask them to think of a topic that they might want more information about and then look it up in the Catechism.

6. Visit the websites of the Vatican and the United States Conference of Catholic Bishops. What topics have been addressed recently? How do they correlate with current events?

7. Talk with younger students about the Commandments of the Church. How can they observe these? Which ones are unfamiliar to them?

CHAPTER 7

This is awesome!

The experience of the sacred

My second graders were all in church for their First Reconciliation. Some were using the confessional and some were using the parish Reconciliation Room. As I meandered through the church, I heard an ungodly yell. One of my dear ones had just left the confessional and was sobbing. Of course I was on the other side of the church, so I literally leapt over pews and kids and whatever else was in my way. When I got there, he was in full pulmonary form; you could have heard him on the moon.

"What happened?" I asked. "Did Father get mad at you?"

> *"For the Son of Man will come like the lightning which flashes across the whole sky from the east to the west."*
>
> MATTHEW 24:27

"No," he sobbed and then wailed.

"Did you forget your act of contrition?" I went on.

"No." By now everyone's attention had been secured.

"Then what happened?"

Hardly able to get the words out, he blubbered, "Father told me to say three Hail Marys and I only know ONE!"

And so it goes.

I believe that there is an innate sense of the mysterious and even the holy in kids. Just look at them play their favorite game. It's a ritual; if you try to change it, they go berserk. It's done *this* way, and if you mess it up, something bad will happen. Whenever I was with my four-year-old niece, I would ask her if she wanted to go to Booger King. "It's BURGER King," she would say, in total exasperation. "Oh, you mean Burgler King," I would reply. She still thinks that I have the intelligence of a cucumber, I'm sure.

I especially liked watching my seventh graders prepare for a test. They constructed shrines on their desks: the little Sacred Heart statue was there, likewise the Blessed Virgin Mary, and maybe St. Joseph. Also present were a favorite Smurf and the lucky rabbit's foot (you can't take any chances).

They are not all that quick to exhale "Awesome!" But when it happens, it's a reminder to us of the ability of a youngster to pause when there is something unexplainable, something in the realm of mystery. I am reminded of the pivotal scene from *The Miracle Worker* in which Annie Sullivan, Helen Keller's teacher, exclaims, "She knows, Mrs. Keller. She KNOWS!" Using this scene to talk about Baptism was a real eye-opener for them; thereafter, they'd look for baptismal scenes in movies and stories. (The famous leap in *Butch Cassidy and the Sundance Kid* comes to mind.)

In this vein, I often encourage teachers and catechists not to dismiss sacramentals. We all need something, literally, to hold on to, and holy cards, holy water fonts, rosaries, scapulars, medals, provide the tangible sign of the intangible. I was a guest speaker for a group of students at the University of Dayton recently. I could not help but notice that so many of them wore scapulars; I thought that scapulars had gone the way of the dinosaur. Each of these students related to me his or her story of being "invested" with the scapular, and how its presence helped them to remember its meaning as a representation of "putting on Christ" (although, historically, it was a form of religious habit for Third Order religious).

We Catholics are great at "stuff"—all the items listed above plus incense, candles, vestments, holy vessels—a veritable treasure-trove of reminders of the sacred. Children who are used to collecting (remember Pokemon cards?) can relate to these representations of what is intangible and invisible. Don't underestimate the gifts of a rosary, a prayer book, a children's Bible, a medal for First Communion, First Penance, Confirmation; these should be special for these special occasions.

Each time I attend the Archdiocese of Los Angeles Religious Education Congress, I am awestruck by the number of teens in tee shirts proudly proclaiming their parish or their church youth group. One of the reasons that teens join gangs is that gangs wear special colors or clothing that both set them apart and integrate them into the group. Let's play into that by our use of sacramentals—and that includes tee shirts, hats, jackets—whatever works.

One of the reasons that I became a Catholic school principal was to have the power to set off the fire alarm for a fire drill. Now, it is generally understood that a fire will never happen in inclement weather. After all, fire drills are only held on nice, sunny, warm days, so why worry when it's raining or snowing?

One wet February school day, the students had just come back from lunch (my students all walked home for lunch). The janitor had just finished mopping the hallways and floors to get rid of the slush that had been tracked in, when the fire alarm went off. As teachers and students made for the exits, they shot withering looks my way: "How dare you pull a fire drill in the middle of winter, in the snow and slush?" I had not pulled a drill and had no idea what had happened. I was calling the fire department, when Arthur, an eighth-grade boy, appeared in my office doorway.

"Sister, we have to talk," he said.

"Not now, Arthur. I am trying to figure out if we have a fire, where it is, and how serious," I replied.

"Sister, we really have to talk," he persisted.

"Not now!"

"But Sister, I did it. I pulled the alarm."

"Sit down," I said. "We need to talk. Why?"

"Well, I noticed that all the fire stations in the school had a glass cover over the button, except one, and I wanted to know if it would work, and it did."

Now I was faced with alerting the fire department to a false alarm and calling everyone back into the school and out of the cold and snow. And, of course, the hallways and floors, so neatly mopped before, were now a mess.

"Arthur, what do you think should happen?" I asked.

"I think I should mop the floors and apologize to everyone."

And so he did.

I came to realize that Arthur had "got it." He realized that an apology was only half the action needed to fix what he had done, and he came up with an adequate way of repairing the breach that his actions had created. I think that Arthur taught me about contrition and penance more than anyone else. What might have been considered merely mischievous became something else, and he rose to the occasion.

Certainly the reflection on the place of God in their lives, the efficacy of prayer, especially communal prayer, and the realization of the little miracles in their lives should be enough to sustain young people. On the efficacy of prayer, I used Garth Brooks' song "Unanswered Prayers" when I taught about the depth of God's love for each of us as individuals, that God *customizes* God's love for individuals. The ballad is about a man who is with his wife at a football game and they run into his old high school sweetheart. He reminisces in his mind how much he had loved her all those years ago, and prayed to God that she would be his for all the rest of his life. But he realizes that God had a greater gift for him: the woman who is his wife and who is standing next to him.

I used to ask the kids about how God answered their prayers without answering their prayers, and they would tell their own stories of the mystery of God's love in their lives. I think it made them feel that God had a personal interest in them, and that this was happening all the time. I think that working with young adolescents, though they can drive you crazy (short ride, that) have that ability to see through the mundane, if only we call their attention to it. So many teachers and catechists don't want to teach sixth, seventh, and eighth graders, because they are so challenging. But they provide for us such a unique experience of the "unfolding" that they go through at this time; I wouldn't miss it for the world.

It seems to me that young people are more introspective than we give them credit for.

There is a phenomenon that has appeared fairly recently. It's the practice of creating roadside "shrines"—markers to commemorate the accidental deaths of individuals on the road. Often I am tempted to stop, examine these memorials, or even to research who these individuals were, how they died, if they left behind a family. Obviously, their loved ones wanted to commemorate their passing, and, perhaps, to caution other drivers that the roads are dangerous.

But it's the urge to create these shrines, these sacred spaces that fascinates me. Churches and chapels are certainly and obviously special and sacred spaces. But there are others. The Romantic poet William Wordsworth ("The Tables Turned") wrote, "One impulse from a vernal wood /can teach you more of man/ of moral evil and of good/than all the sages can." The need to seek the transcendent out of the ordinary is expressed in our youngsters' attitudes toward their personal spaces: their bedrooms, desks, lockers, etc. We can create sacred spaces in our classrooms by including prayer tables, and inviting children to take off their shoes as they approach the prayer table at the beginning of class. Our own behavior as we approach the prayer table, or a special place for reflection will go far in giving young people the idea that even ordinary places can be special.

Many parishes have prayer gardens, or outdoor shrines or Stations of the Cross. Our children can benefit from visiting these and reflecting on their special nature. We can use parish shrines for

May crownings, visits to pray for the intercession of Our Lady, or the special saint whose shrine commemorates a holy life, or a Living Rosary, or the re-enactment of the Stations of the Cross.

Growing up, I worked with my mother every May to create a shrine to Mary. We used the Fatima statue that she had given me at my First Communion, some crepe paper, and lilies of the valley from the garden to create a shrine in my bedroom. It was not only a special time for me and my mother, but it created something very special in my very own room. I was reminded, each time I entered, that there was something that spoke of the transcendent right there in my room. To this day, I create a May shrine in my bedroom. Great practices die hard.

Faced with their daily challenges, our young people need to see beyond what's in front of them: what you see is not what you get. If they have a sense of the mystery of God and of the Church, they will look for it everywhere and when they find it, they'll understand what faith is all about. Their task is not only to grow up but to grow in; the impetuosity of youth must become the energy to drive their "theophanies." Thus can they understand that God works miracles every day.

LESSON

Listen for "awesome."

TRY THIS

1. Ask students to describe their best Christmas. Was it "awesome"?

2. Ask older students to be aware of their breathing, heartbeat, pulse. Then ask them to try to imagine what would happen if they had to think of these things every second. Give them some time to imagine this so as to appreciate God's mindfulness of them.

3. Ask students to bring in some photos that they have taken of memorable places they have been. Have them discuss why these are great photos.

4. Stop class at the first snowfall, or an electrical storm, or a particularly windy day. Discuss what it takes for these phenomena to happen.

5. Construct a bulletin board of truly amazing photos.

6. Build a shrine in the classroom or whatever teaching space is used to commemorate Mary, or Joseph, or the Sacred Heart. Explain to the students the nature and purpose of shrines. Have them study the history of wayside shrines and their use in Europe.

CHAPTER 8

You want me to do what?

Challenges of the faith

Welcome Back, Kotter was a TV comedy that aired during the 1970s. Although it was not a critical success, it provided the acting start for John Travolta, aka Vinnie Barbarino. Every girl wanted to date Vinnie, and every boy wanted to be Vinnie. Vinnie wore what is now called a "mullet"; his hair was combed over from the sides, and he had distinctive sideburns. When Eddie showed up in my class on a Monday with his new Vinnie Barbarino hairstyle, I exclaimed, "You look like John Travolta!" As Eddie basked in this adulation, from the back of the room came, "He looks more like John REvolta!" Very clever, very funny.

> *"Listen! I am sending you out like sheep among wolves."*
>
> MATTHEW 10:16

"By the end of the morning, I want you to apologize to Eddie," I told the offender, "and I'll ask him if you did."

"You want me to do what?" was the rejoinder.

Looking back now, I am sure that my students would have sacrificed their allowance for some cause, spent a Saturday cleaning up someone's yard, even stayed after school to help me. But to restore the harmony of the classroom and their student-to-student relationships? Well that's another matter, and it highlights two principles of Catholic life that should be confronted in our classrooms: the restoration of respect for the community, and the necessity of forgiveness and reconciliation.

Ethicists talk about the restoration of the moral sphere—that when a moral principle has been violated, restitution must be made and the harmony of the community must be repaired. This necessarily entails remorse, forgiveness, and reconciliation, and thus, the real challenge of living as a Catholic Christian can be confronted. In other words, our classrooms need to be places of forgiveness as well as of love and concern. This is a challenge for both the teacher/catechist and the students, but it is at the heart of our faith. One of the last messages that Jesus delivered was about forgiveness, and for many students, this is a hefty challenge. St. Paul writes: "If anyone has given offense, he has hurt not only me, but in some measure, to say no more, every one of you. The punishment already inflicted by the majority on such a one is enough; you should now relent and support him so that he may not be crushed by too great a weight of sorrow. I therefore beg you to reaffirm your love for him" (2 Corinthians 2:5–9).

I always made it a practice to tell my "repeat offenders" that, when they had apologized and served out their sentences, the matter was over. "I am turning over a new page in your life here," I would say, "I won't mention this again, I promise." That really worked; what had dogged their lives was their reputation for trouble. By erasing all that, they now had a chance to create a new present. Too often, our students feel that they have to live up to the nefarious reputations they have accrued, especially when they have traveled with the rest of the class as a cohort over a period of years. Cleaning the slate is a real ray of hope for them.

What seems daunting to youngsters often has been made to be larger than it is. Take Lent: When I told my sixth-grade class that we had to give up something during Lent when I was a kid, they thought that was a neat idea. I thought: Hadn't someone told them about this before? But they came up with a really great project.

We had had some correspondence from our Sisters in Brazil. It seemed that the people in one village needed water purifiers because babies and little children were dying from the tainted water in the river. The water purifiers could be bought for fifty dollars.

My students' idea was that they would give up a movie. So they sold movie "tickets" for eight dollars, the cost of going to a real movie. Each purchaser could write on the "ticket" the movie he or she was giving up, and all the tickets were posted on a bulletin board. By the end of Lent, we had collected over one thousand dollars. They loved it.

It has been said that this generation of youngsters is the most "volunteered" generation ever. While they may seem self-centered, they can be called to great heroism: All they need is a personal invitation, and a face to pin on a "cause." I think that the commercials for the Christian Children's Fund do a great job of that. You see the sad little faces of children in a Latin American slum and are told that a donation of only pennies a day will rescue one of those children from poverty. It really works.

When Hurricane Katrina hit the Gulf Coast of the US, donations were solicited to help people displaced by the tragedy. But Catholic schools and parishes partnered up with parishes and schools in the South and made person-to-person connections. As a result, over one million dollars from children was presented to the Archdiocese of New Orleans to help rebuild those schools and parishes.

I believe that our children need to understand that this faith of ours is not soft or mushy; it's solid and full of personal challenges. Dare a youngster to do something, and he or she will go to the ends of the earth to do it.

I think that this is a good place to bring up the saints. Although a great many of them, both recognized and non-recognized, died for the faith, a great many lived for the faith, and hence might seem more relevant to young people.

One of my all-time favorite books is James Martin's *My Life with the Saints* (2006). Writing about St. Thérèse of Lisieux, Father Martin sums up the essence of sainthood thus:

> It was her deep humility that rendered Thérèse of Lisieux a potent and accessible model for Christians worldwide. After all, who hasn't been humbled by life? Who hasn't experienced personal limitations? Who hasn't felt "little" compared to others? Who hasn't suffered? Thérèse is a saint who many feel would understand their problems. Thérèse is someone an ordinary person can relate to. We feel comfortable with her.

If these words don't define a saint, then our students will never want to get to know one, much less be one.

But the "plaster saints" were, in their lives, flesh and blood. If the lives of some of them seem too removed from the lives of our students, there are still many they can relate to. For example, Sister Ita Ford, Sister Maura Clarke, Sister Dorothy Kazel, and Ms. Jean Donovan were martyred in El Salvador in December 1980. A beautiful movie, *Roses in December*, was produced about their lives and their work, and my students were reduced to tears each time we viewed it. Certainly Dorothy Day, Oscar Romero, Mother Teresa, and Edith Stein are worthy saints for students to study and emulate. Their lives chronicle the marvelous work of God in transforming ordinary people into extraordinary persons. Young people need models of what we mean by saints; we need to look at the good works and holy lives, but also the faults and foibles, warts and wrinkles of people who met the challenge of holiness.

LESSON

Dare to dare.

TRY THIS

1. Invite a missionary to come and speak to the class, or do a PowerPoint presentation. This will put a face on a cause.
2. Discuss several projects with the students. Let them research each of the projects and maybe even visit the sites. Then ask them how they would like to help.
3. Ask students to keep a journal of the challenges to their

faith with which they have been faced. Some examples might be: to sleep in on Sunday instead of going to church, to argue with a sibling, etc. Then ask them to reflect on how they can meet those challenges.

4. Watch the movie *Romero* or *Roses in December* to see how real-life people met the challenges to their faith.

5. Read 2 Corinthians 11:16–33 to the class and ask students to reflect on how they would write those lines from their own experience.

6. Ask students to research Mother Theodore Guerin, Teilhard De Chardin, Anna Dengal, Julian of Norwich, Damien de Veuster, Mary MacKillop, and Franz Jagerstatter on the internet, and then put together a PowerPoint presentation of their findings.

7. Have students put together a list of movies about saints.

CHAPTER 9

A martini in a teacup

People are always telling me "nun jokes." They email me cartoons and photos, send me funny books about nuns, shower me with nun calendars at Christmas, and share nun stories with me. Everyone has a joke about nuns. (I am not a nun; I am a Sister. Nuns take solemn vows and usually stay in cloisters, and sisters take what are known as simple vows and usually are active in an "external" apostolate such as teaching or nursing.)

Here's the joke: A nun, in full habit, is invited out to dinner with a group of people. In the restaurant, the waiter comes to the table and takes the cock-

> *"Who do you say that I am?" Jesus asked. Peter answered, "You are the Messiah."*
>
> MARK 8:29

tail order. When he gets to the nun, he asks, "Sister, would you like a cocktail before dinner?"

"I would love a martini," she replies. "But if you bring me a martini in this restaurant, and everyone sees me, I will give grave scandal. So, can you bring me a martini in a teacup?"

"I'll see what I can do," says the waiter. So, he goes to the bartender, hands in the drink order and says to the bartender, "While you're filling the drink order, can you make me a martini in a teacup?"

The bartender looks up and says, "Is that nun back again?"

Very funny. I use this joke to remind catechists and teachers that they are always a teacher or a catechist. Pope John Paul II said it this way: "Young people don't pay attention to teachers; they pay attention to witnesses. And if they do pay attention to teachers, it is because they are witnesses." The catechist/teacher, then, must not just "talk the talk"; he or she must "walk the walk." When youngsters figure out that we are mouthing pious platitudes but not living them out, we will lose them forever.

Children will frequently bring up to adults their foibles; most are not so artful that they can soften the blow, either. I had students call me on many occasions to point out my failings. "Sister, you told us to be quiet during the fire drill, but you were talking with another teacher during the drill." "Sister, you told us to be prayerful after Communion, but you were talking to the principal." Ouch. I have concluded that they are watching us twenty-four hours a day, just to see if living out of the faith really can be done.

My adolescent students were always confounded by my vows of poverty, chastity, and obedience. "How can you do that?" they'd ask. I had to explain, over and over again, that the vows keep me focused on them. But I have come to the conclusion that it is not just the vowed religious who are poor, chaste, and obedient. Catechists who are single or married carry these evangelical counsels, too, albeit in a different way, and we need to acknowledge that.

Ask any group of Catholic schoolteachers or catechists how many of them are doing what they do for money. They will laugh! Of course not! They so frequently tell me that this is a call, a vocation, and they feel it is their duty to teach, to let the younger generation in on what it is about the Catholic Church that has drawn them.

No, all of us are poor in that our attitude is that of the Beatitude: "Blessed are the poor in spirit." What Jesus is talking about is an attitude of abundance. Where others see nothing, the catechist or Catholic school teacher sees much. That's why catechists are constantly trolling garage sales and junk heaps; you never know: one person's junk is a catechist's treasure. Just think, parish religious education programs and Catholic schools shouldn't exist. After all, we don't have a ton of money, our buildings, in cities especially, are decrepit, and we're still using the front and the back of a piece of paper, and then we consider that the *edges* still have some space left on them.

Catechists and teachers always laugh when I tell them that they have to be chaste. Oftentimes it's because they think I mean *celibate*. No, chastity is simply being honest and true in our relationships, within the context of the state of life one has chosen. I tell them that there cannot be a disconnect between what they present of themselves to their students, and what they live out in their private lives; sooner or later, students will figure it out. And kids don't like hypocrites. Once youngsters figure out that their teacher is a phony, it's all over. Talk the talk *and* walk the walk.

Obedience is simply relying on God to point the way. I tell new teachers that this job is not just a job; it's an opportunity to meet the Holy Spirit, because if they aren't open to what the Spirit is telling them, they won't be inspired teachers who inspire students.

There are countless instances where catechists have told me how they have handled difficult situations, in or out of class. "I don't know where it came from, but I just seemed to say the right thing." Or: "It was just an inspired moment, and the parent said, 'that's just what I needed to hear.'" If that's not the Holy Spirit hovering over the world with ah! bright wings (apologies to G.M. Hopkins), I don't know what is.

It is the witness of these three attributes that will convince our students that we really mean what we teach.

I have come up with a five-fold set of principles for determining whether or not a community exists among catechists or Catholic school teachers:

1. *Everyone understands that he or she has an effect on the bottom line.*

Every institution has a mission statement; it's the "bottom line" of the organization. A mission statement proclaims to the world why the organization exists, and what it does. Often, in the parish religious education program or the Catholic school, people assume that the mission is the administrator's job. But in a community setting, the mission is everyone's job.

Here is an example of a parish mission statement: "Immaculate Conception parish is a Roman Catholic community dedicated to making the Word of God known and loved, creating a community of faith, and doing Christian service to those who need it."

The mission of the Catholic school and of the parish faith formation program have to proceed from this and should reflect it in every deed that is done in each of the programs. But it also means that whether it's the person who prepares youngsters for sacramental programs or the kindergarten teacher, he or she needs to ensure that teaching is geared toward this end.

I frequently run retreat days for teachers and catechists where I ask them to reflect on the mission statement: What does this mean in practical terms to me? How should my actions be geared towards this mission? How do I know when the mission is not being advanced? Can I reflect, at the end of each day, on how I either advanced or impeded the mission today? In the end, it is the actions and words of teachers that matter in a child's life, and not those of the administrator.

2. Dirty laundry is kept where it should be.

Occasionally we all have a bad day and think that we will feel better about ourselves if we spread the misery around. And so, we find ourselves griping or complaining in a place and to people who really should not witness it. First of all, this kind of whining vitiates point one above. Second, real communities see that negative words about the community tear that community apart.

If students or parents or even other teachers or catechists spoil our usual euphoria, we need to vent where it's appropriate—the administrator's office, or the faculty room or someplace where it will stay in-house. Neither students nor parents need to know that we were ticked off about something. When I ask teachers about their own children, they can't tell me enough about how handsome or beautiful or intelligent or talented they are. What they don't tell me about is the argument they had with a teenage daughter that morning, or how worried they are about their nine-year-old son who has started refusing to go to church. Keep dirty laundry in the closet where it belongs.

3. People fill in for each other in times of absence.

On June 18, 2009, on a flight from Belgium to the United States, the pilot died while the plane was somewhere over the Atlantic Ocean. The co-pilot immediately took over the plane's controls, and a reserve co-pilot, sitting in the passenger section, came to the flight deck and took the co-pilot's place. Passengers were unaware of any trouble until they disembarked in New York. Their take on this sad incident was "The crew was professional to the core." And "We never knew what was happening; the service was seamless." Here was a real tragedy for the flight crew, yet, mindful of their responsibility to passengers, they stifled their own feelings and continued to deliver on their promise of service. What a great example!

At one point in my career, I moderated the glee club. I thought this would be fun; after all, it had *glee*. I soon found that teen girls don't eat for weeks before a concert; they might look fat, even though they wore these huge choir robes. And so, I always had someone fainting during a performance.

So, I told them, if someone faints, lower her to the risers and then fill in the "hole" with your choir robes.

It often happens that someone doesn't show up, or someone doesn't deliver whatever it was that he or she promised, and the event or project or whatever can be ruined. The real community delivers seamless service because that is what youngsters deserve of us. As a principal, I was always having teachers call in sick or having to leave because one of their own children needed them. I was fortunate in having a very generous faculty that would "fill in" when needed. Moreover, I took the opportunity of substituting for them, because it gave me great insights into what was really happening in classrooms.

As a catechist, I experienced numerous occasions when another catechist didn't show up. My kids loved it when I would simply combine my class with the students of the missing teacher. The kids reflected the pride they took in their class when they showed our "guests" around and introduced them to our routines.

In Luke's Gospel (10:17–20), the seventy-two disciples return from their journey of spreading the good news. They are bragging about what they did, but Jesus rebukes them and reminds them of who worked through them; they are mere instruments of the work of God. This is the attitude we need, to understand that the world neither stands nor falls because of us, but that our job is to see to it that we deliver the goods to youngsters.

4. People pray regularly for and with each other.

I felt so bad about kids who were in places where they could not pray publicly on September 11, 2001, especially in New York City.

What a great opportunity we had in Catholic schools and in our religious education programs to assuage young children's fears by modeling the community at prayer. It was a comfort to both children and adults and confirmed the practice of prayer as a firm principle behind the presence of a community.

How many times have we been asked to pray for another teacher, or a parent, or a spouse or child, or whatever? Think of this supportive prayer as the cement that binds the community of the school or the religious education program or the youth ministry program together. We need to remind ourselves that we work in and through a community of faith, and not a social network, or a common-interest club.

Prayer together before we begin teaching, an annual day of recollection or a retreat, or letting someone in distress or sorrow know that you are presenting their needs to God in prayer, are huge affirmations of the importance of prayer in the lives of the community.

People often think that, because I am a vowed religious, I have some kind of "in" with God, and so they frequently beseech me to pray for something. (Of course I tell them I'll pray as long as they do, too). I live in a large apartment complex, and, when one of the office personnel told me about her twenty-two-year-old nephew who is fighting cancer, I told her I would write to him and let him know that I was praying for him.

A couple of days later, he called his aunt to tell her what a thrill it was to get a card (and I had found a holy card of his patron, St. Matthias, and included it) and my message and promise of prayer. I believe that this is what we mean by the Communion of Saints, and a community that regularly prays exemplifies that.

5. People have fun together.

It's the fun times that we remember, and every family has those funny stories, like "remember when Grandpa sneezed and his teeth flew across the room and hit Grandma?" Likewise, every school I ever worked in had its legends—those hilarious moments, the very mention of which brings gales of laughter.

Social events, birthday parties, parties for no good reason, should all be planned during the year. When we let our hair down we can begin to get beyond the perfunctory "hello" or "how are you" without waiting for an answer. I think that when the first four principles are in place, especially principle four, the fun will come effortlessly. After all, a real community is a place where we want to go, and it's the fun that is not only the reward for work well done, but is the real stepping-off point for the deepening of community.

One of my favorite teaching experiences was at an all-girls' high school. We had about eighty on the faculty and staff, and annually held a family picnic. We had games for children and adults and children/adults, water balloon tosses, watermelon seed spitting contests—you get the picture. Finally, we had a cookout that included side dishes and desserts contributed by each of the staff members. Those picnics offered the opportunity to meet spouses and "significant others" and to watch the kids grow and mature as the years went on. Even to this day (and that was over twenty years ago), when I meet one of those teachers, I can inquire after spouse and kids by name, and I think I had a better understanding of the teachers and staff members as I talked and played with their families.

The National Federation for Catholic Youth Ministry, the National Association for Lay Ministry, and the National Conference for Catechetical Leadership have collaborated to produce *National Certification Standards for Lay Ecclesial Ministers* (2003). It's a document that explores five standards that reflect the ministerial competence of parish ministers who are not ordained.

They are: Personal and Spiritual Maturity, Lay Ecclesial Ministry Identity, Catholic Theology, Pastoral Praxis, and Professional Practice. Under each of the standards is a set of competencies required for youth ministers, catechetical directors, pastoral associates, and parish life coordinators. I am no proponent of the current craze over standardization, but this document provides to the aforementioned persons something to be attained, an ideal to be sought, and a direction as to the kind of knowledge and practice that should be expected of a lay minister in the Church.

What we do is not merely a volunteer or a ministry opportunity. What we do is fundamental to the passing on of this wonderful gift we have been given: our Catholic faith. While our students may not remember the intricacies of the Catechism, or the Beatitudes, or even the liturgical seasons, they will remember us. We are, therefore, in the business of making memories. And those memories will either serve our students as they journey in their faith life, or they will cut that journey short.

LESSON

This is risky business.

TRY THIS

1. Make sure that there is a faculty retreat offered at least once a year. Use that time to reflect on the mission statement of the school and parish, and ask each individual to write his or her own personal mission statement.

2. Ask each catechist to keep a journal in which the catechist can record those significant times in the classroom where a personal theophany has taken place.

3. Have students ask their parents or grandparents to relate to them stories of their favorite teachers. Collect these and ask students what qualities their parents or grandparents admired in their teachers. Then have them discuss how they will cultivate these qualities in their own lives.

4. Have students be "teacher for a day." What qualities of their own teachers did they pick up on? Idiosyncrasies? Negative qualities? (Sometimes our students tell us about ourselves when they act out our jobs.)

5. Ask teachers and catechists to write their personal mission statement; how does it match that of the parish? The Church?

CHAPTER 10

Meet the parents

When I ask teachers and catechists, "Who would prefer to teach orphans?" they all raise their hands. They tell me, over and over, "it's not the kids; it's the parents."

Now the "it," I think, is the trouble that anyone who has anything to do with young people sooner or later confronts. Today's parents are not the parents of yore; there is something else going on, and for the youth minister or the catechist or the Catholic schoolteacher, that's what's so hard to handle.

I often regale groups of catechists and teachers alike with my

> *"A Jewish official came to him, knelt down before him and said, 'My daughter has just died; but come and place your hands on her and she will live.'"*
>
> MATTHEW 9:18

stories of my first years of teaching. I had a self-contained (I taught everything, including art and music) class of forty-eight sixth graders. Then, after school on Tuesday, I had fifty sixth graders for religious education), and on Wednesday I had thirty high school sophomores. My audience laughs, a little nervously: it can't be done. Well, it could be done then because parents were unquestionably in my corner. If I had to call a parent about a student's untoward behavior, I knew that the parent would back me up.

Here's how it went: "Hello, Mrs. Webster, I am Sister Carol, Bobby's teacher."

"Bobby! You come right over here! What did he do, Sister?" After I read the indictment, the parent would say: "Don't worry, Sister, it will never happen again." And I knew that she was right.

Here's how it goes now: "Hello Mrs. Webster-Jones; I am Sister Carol, Kyle's teacher."

Parent: "Do you have any proof that he did that? Is there forensic evidence? Someone else made him do it. Does he need a lawyer? I told him, 'If someone hits you, hit him back; in fact, take a preemptive strike and hit him first.'"

And so it goes.

To be fair, parents are at sea when it comes not only to raising their kids, but to teaching and modeling the faith. This generation of parents did not get good, solid grounding in the Catholic faith, even if they attended Catholic school. Remember the '60s and '70s? We were teaching a backlash of the '50s recital of the Baltimore Catechism; from an all-head approach we swung the other way to all "heart," and so religion class consisted of launching balloons, creating collages, and discussing how Jesus loves you, without any serious discussion about tenets, the creed, morality, or the history of the Catholic Church. Result: Generations X and Y, and now they have children of their own.

Here's how I comfort parents: In the Gospel of Matthew we read that Mary and Joseph took Jesus to Jerusalem, as was their custom, when he was twelve years old. Here's how it went:

They're returning to Nazareth and Mary says to Joseph, "Where is he?"

Joseph replies, "He was with you."

Mary counters, " I asked you to keep an eye on him."

Joseph says, "No, he went with the women."

Mary says, "You lost the son of God?"

They return to Jerusalem, find Jesus in the Temple, and he gives them a hard time: "Did you not know that I must be doing my father's business?"

"You're coming with us, young man," counter Mary and Joseph. And thus, we hear nothing of Jesus for the next eighteen years, because he has been grounded for staying out all night without permission.

There has been a great deal of study of this generation of parents, and what makes them tick. The consensus is that they are a different lot from their parents, the Baby Boomers and my generation, called "the Silent Generation." (hmph!) Here's what Laurence Steinberg (2005) says: "Baby boomers are often called 'helicopter parents…their high expectations actually are setting up their children for disappointment." The next generation, according to Nancy Robinson (2006), has never lived without computers and other technology, and expect it to be used in every situation. They expect that their children will be confident not seeking information from adults, but finding anything they wish to know online.

The current generation of parents, born between 1965 and 1980, is highly educated (twenty-nine percent have a college degree, more than the general US population), were raised to be independent, are used to solving problems, are entrepreneurial by nature, and want to be more involved in their own children's lives than their own parents were. They are a people in search of a community, according to Robert Bellah (1994), and want a cause around which to rally and pour out their energy. They are busy, belong to many organizations, and are used to short-term, rather than long-term solutions to problems. (That's why they resist having to come to meetings, and programs in order to have their children receive the sacraments). While I can commiserate with them, however, the journey of a parent with a child toward a sacrament is priceless.

There is so much information available on parents and parenting, but I offer, below, some ideas on dealing with them, and engaging them to truly be the primary educators of their children.

LESSON

Understand that parents are at sea when it comes to raising their children in the faith; help them to do this.

TRY THIS

1. Remember that this generation of parents is trying to be better than their own parents. They have seen their parents divorce or move away, and they don't want to do that to their families. Therefore they are looking for answers to the question: How do I become the ideal parent? While there

is no pat answer, the fact that the question is asked is pivotal. I would suggest that schools and parishes do all they can to help parents with parenting.

2. Host a Sunday afternoon of recollection with parents. Take care of the kids in another place, so that the parents are not preoccupied with the kids. Just a few hours of reflection on any number of spiritual topics, with some time for prayer and dialogue would go a long way toward helping busy parents with their spiritual lives.

3. Make sure that parents have a list of expectations of the program or the school. At the very least, they should expect that their child will receive good instruction, that values will be integrated into all parts of the program, that their child will be known as an individual, that the school or the parish will establish good lines of communication, and that issues that arise will be dealt with in collaboration with parents.

4. On the other hand, teachers and catechists should expect support for their decisions, parental help with assignments (not doing them, but helping), that children know their prayers before they come to class, and that parents will take the kids to church on the weekend.

5. Teachers and catechists at various levels should lend their expertise. For example, the early childhood teachers can write some articles on preparing your child to attend religion classes, helping your child to pray. Middle level teachers can write about helping your young adolescent through a tough time in his or her growing up, talking to your young teen about God, encouraging the young teen to attend

Mass. Junior high and high school teachers can discuss helping your teen through adolescence, what to do when your teen tells you he hates God and you, keeping your teen connected with the Church, sharing your own faith stories with your teenager, and what to say when your teen asks you about your youth.

In short, we need to involve parents throughout their children's religious development. They need to understand the teachings of the Church and we can help them. Most important, they need to stay involved in their children's lives, even when their teens are pulling away. If we are to pay more than lip service to the priority that parents have in educating their children, then we must take the initiative in their children's spiritual formation by helping the adults with their own spirituality.

AFTERWORD

Eight physical elements
...That make a huge difference in the classroom

Teachers and catechists are confronted with their own challenges these days. One of the most daunting is facing a group of young people on a regular basis, either daily or weekly. Talk with anyone who has been teaching for more than twenty years, and he or she will tell you that kids are not the same today as they were in yesteryear. Anyone who teaches youngsters needs to pay attention to this.

I frequently present a workshop entitled "Everything They Didn't Teach You in College." It is a potpourri of lessons that I have learned from teaching. Teachers report that one of the most useful parts of this presentation is the exploration of physical factors that relate to student behavior in the classroom or whatever setting is used for instruction. Here is a list of factors, and some remedies, that instructors have found useful.

1. Weather Students find it very difficult to concentrate when the setting is too hot or too cold; everyone acknowledges that. But windy weather is just as disconcerting to youngsters. The constant movement of trees, dust, whatever, outside the windows is distracting. Close the blinds or the drapes, or whatever you have; it will block out the noise and the distracting movements. A falling barometer presages a storm, but it also adversely affects student behavior. Use stormy days for a review of past learning.

2. Light Some young people are very sensitive to fluorescent lights; so are you, especially when the bulb is beginning to die. Seat these youngsters away from the lights, or, better still, on a sunny day don't turn on the lights at all.

3. Open/closed Similar to the light factor, some youngsters are more comfortable in either a closed space or an open space within the learning environment. Think: where do you like to sit in a restaurant: a table or a booth? Most adults prefer a booth; hey, it's enclosed, cozy, intimate, whatever. Also, restaurants are usually darkened with indirect lighting at night—a nice, comfortable, relaxing atmosphere. Think about it—what are your students' preferences?

4. Color Whatever made us think that using red, orange, and yellow in the classroom was wise? Research has shown that these are arousing colors. Several years ago, the University of Wisconsin tried painting classrooms pale yellow or pale green. You guessed it: Students reported feeling more relaxed, calmer. Watch for visual over-stimulation. Remember the last time you were in a retail store and there was too much "stuff" around and it was crowded with racks and tables of merchandise? Wasn't it confusing?

5. Noise The adage goes: "Music hath charms to soothe the savage breast" (or beast in some versions—depends on your attitude towards kids, I guess). This generation of young people is constantly plugged in to an iPod, or some version thereof, listening to music, or to what passes for music. Good liturgical music, ballads, even, heaven forefend, some Enya found their way into my classes. Check out chapter one again on the musical intelligence, and remember that even elevator music is there to calm, soothe, and to help us reflect.

6. Smell Many years ago, I noticed that, as my plane was landing, a floral scent was filling the cabin of the airplane. When I inquired about this, I was told that the scent was used to calm passengers, especially first-time flyers. Aromatherapy is a multi-million dollar business, and retailers use it to good advantage (try passing a Cinnabon without at least musing about buying one). When my students were hard to calm down, or especially antsy (like around Christmas time), I would use a plug-in room deodorizer. Floral scents and citrus scents have a soothing effect; that's why they don't make Barbecue Pledge.

7. Seating Mindful that many religious education classes do not take place in a formal classroom setting, I think that where students park themselves is relevant to this discussion. We often place our "troublemakers" right in front of us, so that we can watch their every move, but is this really the place for them? Every room has a "sweet spot"; it's that area upon which our gaze most frequently falls. Put the kids whom you need to keep an eye on there. As to who sits up front, think of the kids who are a little reluctant to participate, who are always on the wrong page, or give an answer that would be correct for a different question. Put them where you can encourage them, affirm them, make them comfortable—right up front.

8. Sensory preference We have five senses, but, most often, three find themselves in the instructional setting: touch, hearing, and seeing. When it comes to hearing or seeing, most teachers agree that this is a very visual generation. Whereas we used to listen to music, they now have music videos. They have been raised with over 500 television channels, and Facebook, YouTube, texting, and who knows what's next? It's all visual, and we need to meet that preference. I strongly encourage the use of LCD projectors, videos, SmartBoards, and the like. Of course, they will listen to stories, but these have to have some visual link; otherwise, their attention will stray and you will have lost them.

If we pay attention to these seemingly innocuous factors, we can provide a setting for learning. These are not so much challenges of the faith, as challenges of the faithful.

REFERENCES

Armstrong, T. *Multiple Intelligences in the Classroom*. Alexandria, VA: Association for Supervision and Curriculum Development, 1995.

Bellah, R., Madson, W. et al. *Habits of the Heart*. Berkeley, CA: University of California Press, 1996.

Gardner, H.E. *Frames of Mind*. Cambridge, MA: Harvard Business School Press, 1983.

Jacob, K. "U Mass." *US Catholic* 74(7) 37-38, July 2009.

Martin, J. *My Life with the Saints*. Chicago: Loyola Press, 2007.

National Association for Lay Ministry. *National Certification Standards for Lay Ecclesial Ministers*. Washington, DC: NALM, 2007.

Robinson, N. *Iconoculture*. Minneapolis, MN: Iconoculture Organization, 2006.

Steinberg, L. *The Ten Basic Principles of Good Parenting*. New York: Simon and Schuster, 2005.

Taffel, R. *The Second Family*. New York: St. Martin's Press, 2001.